A BUSINESS APPROACH TO CELERY FARMING

Complete Entrepreneurial Step By Step Guide To Celery Garden From Scratch

ZHURI HART

DISCLAIMER

This book is intended to provide general information and insights on adopting a business approach to farming. The content within is based on the author's knowledge and experiences up to the date of publication. It is essential to recognize that the field of agriculture is dynamic, influenced by various factors such as market conditions, climate, and regulatory changes.

Readers are advised to conduct thorough research, seek professional advice, and consider their unique circumstances before implementing any strategies or practices discussed in this book. The author and publisher disclaim any responsibility for the accuracy, completeness, or suitability of the information provided. The book is not a substitute for professional advice, and the author and publisher shall not be liable for any damages or losses arising from the use or reliance on the information presented herein.

Individual results may vary, and success in farming enterprises is contingent upon numerous variables. The author encourages readers to consult with relevant experts, agricultural extension services, and legal or financial professionals to tailor strategies to their specific needs and local conditions.

This book is not intended to be a comprehensive guide to all aspects of farming, and readers should exercise their judgment and discretion in applying the principles discussed. The author and publisher do not endorse any specific products, services, or companies mentioned in this book unless explicitly stated.

By reading this book, the reader acknowledges and accepts the inherent uncertainties in agricultural endeavors and agrees to use the information at their own risk.

TABLE OF CONTENTS

ABOUT THE BOOK

For anyone looking to enter the celery farming sector or improve their operations, the book "A Business Approach to Celery Farming" is a priceless resource. This book covers the essential elements of celery farming, farm setup, business planning, legal issues, marketing tactics, and new trends through a thorough examination of all relevant topics. Its importance stems from its capacity to combine real-world knowledge with a calculated commercial strategy.

The background information about celery farming is given in the introduction, along with an explanation of its goals, extent, and target market. This gives readers a basic overview of the industry and its possibilities. A comprehensive understanding is ensured by the synopsis of the celery growing sector, which also sets the stage for the upcoming chapters.

The book explores the nuances of growing celery. It provides a summary of the botanical world, information on climate and soil needs, suggestions for variety selection, and step-by-step instructions for the germination of seeds, crop planning, and rotation. This is essential information for anyone hoping to succeed in the celery farming industry.

The book then moves on to discuss the practical aspects of starting a celery farm, including where to put the farm, how to build it, what equipment and infrastructure to use, how to handle pests and diseases, and how to use organic farming methods. These realizations are crucial to the effective and long-term running of a celery farm.

Turning now to company planning and strategy, the following section covers financial predictions, risk management, business model development, market research, and audience targeting. This is a critical strategic approach for anyone looking to grow celery as well as start and maintain a successful business in the sector.

The book is devoted to legal and regulatory issues, stressing the significance of permits, licensing, environmental compliance, and upholding quality and safety standards. This legal base is essential for negotiating the regulatory environment and guaranteeing a morally and legally compliant celery farming enterprise.

After that, the book delves into marketing and sales tactics, encompassing topics like customer connection building, branding, packaging, distribution methods, and sales strategies. For any agricultural enterprise to succeed and expand, efficient marketing and sales are essential, and this section offers celery producer's practical advice.

The seventh section covers harvesting and post-harvest management, including the best times and methods for harvesting as well as post-harvest handling, storage, and quality control procedures. By doing this, the reputation and financial success of the celery farm are protected and the final product is guaranteed to retain its quality from the field to the market.

The book which concentrates on new developments and trends, offers readers a forward-looking viewpoint. The exploration of subjects like technological integration, sustainable methods, and keeping up with industry trends equips the reader to flourish in a constantly changing and dynamic celery farming environment.

"A Business Approach to Celery Farming" is an invaluable resource for both novice and seasoned cultivators of celery. It is positioned as the go-to reference for anyone hoping to develop and maintain a successful celery farming business in addition to cultivating celery due to its thorough treatment of business strategy, legal issues, marketing, and developing trends.

CHAPTER ONE

CELERY FARMING INTRODUCTION

SYNOPSIS OF THE CELERY FARMING SECTOR

The agricultural environment is significantly influenced by the celery farming industry, which also boosts local and international economies. The vegetable celery (Apium graveolens) is a popular and adaptable food that is known for its unique flavor and crisp texture. This introduction explores several celery farming facets, offering a thorough synopsis of the sector and the essential components of celery production.

KNOWING HOW TO CULTIVATE CELERY

Understanding the botanical traits, environmental needs, and agricultural techniques of celery is essential to its careful cultivation. According to a botanical overview, celery belongs to the Apiaceae family, which is distinguished by its distinctively fragrant leaves and green stalks.

A plant's life cycle, growth patterns, and distinctive characteristics must be understood for successful cultivation.

CONDITIONS OF THE SOIL AND CLIMATE

Climate and soil quality are two major environmental factors that have a direct impact on the effectiveness of celery growing. Celery needs chilly temperatures to flourish at its best and is found in temperate climates. Because the plant is sensitive to high temperatures, it is important to carefully evaluate the local climate to create an ideal growing habitat. Furthermore, soil quality is crucial; the production of celery requires well-drained, nutrient-rich soils.

DIFFERENT CELERY VARIETIES

Due to the diversity among the species of celery, many variants that are suited to varied growing environments and tastes have been developed. Farmers who want to adjust to local conditions or satisfy specific market demands must understand these cultivars.

Farmers can choose from a variety of alternatives to meet their specific needs, as each variety may have differences in size, flavor, and resistance to disease.

The careful selection and germination of seeds is the first step in the growth of celery. Good genetic traits and high-quality seeds are essential for a successful crop. To give the celery plants a good start, the ideal circumstances for seed sprouting must be created during the germination period. The basis for a healthy crop is laid during this early period of seedling care and management.

CROP ROTATION AND PLANNING

Planning your crops and rotating them is crucial to growing celery sustainably. To fulfill market demands and maximize yields, farmers must carefully consider when to plant and harvest their crops. Crop rotation involves changing up the crops cultivated in a given field to reduce the risk of soil-borne illnesses and preserve soil fertility.

Exploring the celery farming sector requires a comprehensive grasp of botanical elements, climate factors, soil needs, and production techniques. Having a general understanding of these fundamental ideas will enable farmers to successfully plant celery and add to the vibrant and ever-changing agricultural industry.

CHAPTER TWO

PUTTING YOUR CELERY FARM IN ORDER

FARM LAYOUT & DESIGN

The success of your celery farm greatly depends on the site you choose. Celery grows best on soil that drains properly and gets lots of sunlight. Select a location that enjoys direct sunshine for the majority of the day. The soil should also have strong water retention qualities, be rich in organic content, and be fertile. For easier irrigation and farming, a level or gently sloping landscape is ideal. To expedite the distribution process, take into account the market's and the transportation hub's closeness.

Optimizing the structure of your celery farm is crucial to achieving maximum productivity and efficiency. Arrange the beds and rows such that planting, harvesting, and maintenance tasks may be done with ease. Crop rotation techniques can be used to control soil fertility and lower the risk of illness.

To encourage air circulation and reduce the chance of fungal infections, make sure there is enough space between plants.

FACILITIES AND GEAR

A celery farm must be established with the proper infrastructure and equipment, which requires investment.

It could be essential to utilize shade structures or greenhouses to regulate the temperature and shield plants from harsh weather. Setting up a soil preparation area that is favorable for celery development requires the use of high-quality plows and tillers.

Automated planting and harvesting equipment can drastically save labor costs and boost efficiency for large-scale commercial enterprises. Sufficient storage spaces, like refrigerated rooms or warehouses, are essential for maintaining the freshness of harvested celery.

Put in place a dependable irrigation system to guarantee constant moisture levels, and think about adding a drip irrigation system for targeted watering.

WATER MANAGEMENT SYSTEMS

As a crop that requires a lot of water, celery requires an effective irrigation system to thrive to its full potential. For celery farms, drip irrigation is a common option since it minimizes water waste and lowers the danger of foliar infections by providing water straight to the base of the plants.

To guarantee that the crops receive clean water, think about putting in a well-planned irrigation network with suitable filtering equipment.

Keep a regular eye on the moisture content of the soil and modify your irrigation schedule according to the celery's growth stage and the surrounding conditions. Mulching the area around the plants can also aid in weed suppression and soil moisture retention. In addition to promoting healthy plant growth, appropriate water management helps avoid problems like celery stalk breaking.

MANAGEMENT OF DISEASES AND PESTS

Creating a thorough plan to manage pests and diseases is essential to protecting your celery crop. Use integrated pest management (IPM) techniques that incorporate cultural norms, biological control, and sparing chemical use. Keep an eye out for pest indicators on plants regularly, and use beneficial insects and other natural predators to keep pest numbers under control.

Crop rotation is a useful technique for upsetting pest life cycles and lowering the danger of soil-borne illnesses. Maintain a tidy farm environment and get rid of any plant trash right away to get rid of possible insect and disease breeding grounds. Keep a close eye on the weather because certain diseases are more likely to flourish in certain climates. Modify management strategies as necessary.

ORGANIC AGRICULTURE METHODS

Adopting organic farming techniques can improve your celery farm's viability and marketability. Choose organic alternatives to synthetic insecticides and fertilizers. Increase the fertility and structure of your soil by adding compost and other organic amendments. Use cover crops to reduce weeds and increase biodiversity.

Reduce the need for chemical interventions by promoting natural predators and beneficial organisms to manage insect populations. To protect the ecosystem and preserve this valuable resource, manage water resources responsibly. Obtain an organic certification for your celery farm to gain access to higher-end marketplaces and draw in eco-aware customers.

A celery farm's ability to succeed depends on several elements being carefully taken into account, from choosing the best location to putting sustainable and effective farming techniques into practice. Establishing a successful celery farm that is environmentally friendly and productive may be achieved by taking care of pest and disease management, irrigation systems, infrastructure and equipment, farm location and design, and organic farming practices.

CHAPTER THREE

PLANNING AND STRATEGY FOR BUSINESSES

ANALYSIS AND RESEARCH ON THE MARKET

Any effective business plan or strategy is built upon the foundation of market research and analysis. Understanding the dynamics of the market, locating possible rivals, and spotting new trends all depend on conducting in-depth market research. This entails obtaining and analyzing information on consumer preferences, market size, and economic factors. Businesses can get insightful information through thorough analysis, which helps them make decisions and customize their goods and services to fit the needs of niche markets.

CHOOSING YOUR AUDIENCE'S TARGET

The proper audience must be identified and targeted as a crucial component of strategic company strategy.

Businesses may more effectively customize their marketing messages and product offerings when they have a thorough understanding of the needs, tastes, and behaviors of their target audience.

By using demographic, psychographic, and behavioral segmentation, companies can develop focused advertising strategies that appeal to particular clientele groups. This strategy guarantees a better return on investment by optimizing marketing efforts and improving customer interaction.

DEVELOPMENT OF BUSINESS MODELS

A clear business model acts as a road map for how an organization generates, provides, and acquires value. Clarifying the value proposition, comprehending the revenue streams, and identifying the crucial tasks, materials, and collaborations needed for success are all part of building a strong business model. To remain flexible in a fast-paced business climate, companies must constantly review and adjust their business models, whether they are using conventional models or novel strategies like platform models or subscription-based services.

BUDGETS AND FINANCIAL PROJECTIONS

Strategic company planning includes budgeting and financial predictions as essential elements that offer a path to financial success. Forecasting income, costs, and profitability over a given time frame helps businesses make decisions and prove to stakeholders that they are financially stable. Budgeting guarantees that the company maintains its financial discipline and aids in the effective allocation of resources. It entails determining the main causes of costs, defining reasonable goals for revenue, and creating backup strategies to reduce monetary risks.

RISK CONTROL

In the ever-changing corporate world, successful risk management is essential to long-term success. Potential risks must be identified, their impact evaluated, and methods for response or mitigation must be developed by businesses. This includes hazards related to finances, operations, markets, and external variables like shifts in regulations or developments in geopolitics. By putting risk management procedures into place, companies may strengthen their resilience, safeguard their resources, and overcome obstacles with more efficiency. To respond to changing market conditions and new threats, risk management methods must be reviewed and adjusted regularly.

All-encompassing approach that incorporates market research, audience targeting, business model development, financial predictions, and risk management is necessary for effective business planning and strategy. These interdependent components enable companies to make well-informed decisions, adjust to shifting market conditions, and lay the groundwork for sustained long-term growth and viability.

CHAPTER FOUR

REGULATORY AND LEGAL ASPECTS

PERMITS AND LICENSES

Regarding legal and regulatory matters, licenses and permissions are essential for guaranteeing the authenticity and adherence of a celery farming enterprise. Getting the required licenses and permits is a crucial first step for business owners who want to work in agriculture. These licenses, which are intended to control and observe different facets of the farming enterprise, are normally issued by municipal, state, or federal agencies, contingent upon the jurisdiction.

A thorough application that describes the celery farming business, its location, and its adherence to regulations and standards is typically required as part of the licensing procedure. Plans for water use, environmental impact evaluations, and other pertinent papers may be included in this. Legal repercussions, penalties, and even the termination of the farming enterprise may result from the failure to get the necessary licenses and permissions.

RESPECT FOR ENVIRONMENTAL REGULATIONS

Like every agricultural practice, celery growing has an impact on the environment. Adherence to environmental standards is crucial to minimize adverse effects on adjacent communities, ecosystems, and water supplies. Regulations about the environment may cover topics including trash disposal, pesticide application, soil conservation, and water use. These rules must be followed by farmers to encourage ethical and sustainable farming methods.

The use of ecologically sustainable practices, such as organic farming and precision farming, can improve adherence to these rules. To show continued conformity to the established standards, environmental activities may also need to be regularly monitored and reported on. Ensuring environmental compliance not only guarantees the longevity of the celery farming industry but also cultivates a favorable reputation within the community and among environmentally aware consumers.

STANDARDS FOR QUALITY AND SAFETY

Upholding strict safety and quality standards is essential in the celery farming industry. To protect the health and welfare of consumers, strict restrictions apply to the manufacturing, packaging, and distribution of agricultural products. Adherence to good agricultural practices (GAP), which cover the correct handling, storing, and transportation of celery, is one of the quality control measures. These regulations are in place to reduce the possibility of contamination and disease outbreaks and to guarantee that consumers receive fruit that is both safe and nutrient-rich.

A celery farming company can demonstrate its dedication to upholding and surpassing industry standards by putting in place quality management systems and taking part in certification programs.

To ensure the safety of the celery crop, regular testing for pesticides, pollutants, and pathogens is necessary. Noncompliance with these requirements could lead to legal consequences, harm to the company's image, and possible health hazards for customers.

INSURANCE FOR BUSINESSES THAT GROW CELERY

An essential part of risk management for companies engaged in celery farming is insurance. With weather-related disasters, crop diseases, and market changes among the inherent uncertainties in agriculture, it is imperative to have adequate insurance coverage to guard against potential losses. A variety of hazards are usually covered by farm insurance, such as crop failure, property damage, liability for farm accidents, and business interruption.

Specialized coverage for perishable crops and equipment failures may also be included in insurance for celery-growing operations. Farmers must carefully evaluate their own needs and collaborate with insurance companies that are aware of the particular difficulties facing the agriculture industry. In addition to protecting the company's financial stability, adequate insurance gives farmers comfort in the face of the unpredictability of their industry.

CHAPTER FIVE

SALES AND MARKETING

CREATING A NAME FOR YOUR CELERY FARM:

In the field of agriculture, where goods are frequently turned into commodities, branding is essential to differentiating a celery farm from its rivals. Developing a unique farm character that extends beyond the product itself is part of branding.

This can contain a distinctive tagline, logo, and visual and messaging style that are all consistent. This could entail highlighting organic farming methods, sustainability, or any other standout features that appeal to customers for a celery farm.

Developing a gripping narrative is another essential component of a successful celery farm brand strategy. This could entail showcasing the farm's background, the hard work of its farmers, or its passion for offering premium, regionally sourced celery.

A celery farm can build a relationship with customers through effective branding, which will encourage loyalty and raise the perceived worth of its products.

PRESENTATION AND PACKAGING

Packaging is an essential component of the entire product presentation, serving a purpose beyond just holding and safeguarding the vegetables. Packaging for a celery farm should communicate important information to customers and be consistent with the existing brand identity. For instance, using sustainable packaging might highlight the farm's dedication to eco-friendly operations.

The way celery is displayed in marketplaces or supermarkets affects how customers perceive it as well. Purchase decisions might be influenced by attractive displays, cleanliness, and freshness.

Careful attention to detail can improve the overall visual appeal of a product and attract more potential customers. Examples of this include using visually good packaging and appealingly arranging celery.

CHANNELS OF DISTRIBUTION

To effectively reach its target market, a celery farm must carefully consider its distribution networks. Options span from contemporary internet platforms to conventional establishments like supermarkets and farmers' markets. Every channel has a unique set of benefits and difficulties. Grocery stores have a wider audience, but farmers' markets offer a direct line to customers.

A celery farm may reach a larger consumer base through online channels and offer the convenience of home delivery. However, successful distribution depends on having a solid understanding of the requirements and logistics of each channel. The distribution plan can also be adjusted by forming alliances with merchants or investigating direct-to-consumer options, guaranteeing that celery reaches customers most practically and economically.

FORMULATING A SALES APPROACH

Understanding the target market, researching rivals, and determining unique selling propositions are all essential components of a strong sales strategy. This can entail carrying out market research to ascertain consumer preferences, brand-consistent pricing schemes, and distribution networks for a celery farm. Reiterating the farm's dedication to sustainability, freshness, and quality can be an important components of the sales pitch.

To encourage purchases, the sales strategy should also take into account promotional activities like discounts, bundling possibilities, or loyalty programs. In addition, a well-trained sales force and clear contact with distribution partners are necessary to guarantee that the goods of the celery farm are adequately marketed and represented in the marketplace.

CHAPTER SIX

HARVESTING AND MANAGING AFTER HARVEST

IDEAL TIME FOR HARVESTING

One of the most important aspects of agriculture is figuring out when to harvest to get the best quality and yield of produce. varying crops have varying harvest times, which are determined by variables like crop maturity, weather, and intended use. When it comes to fruits and vegetables, picking them at the optimal time guarantees maximum flavor, maximum nutritional value, and maximum market value.

To determine the ideal harvesting period, farmers sometimes rely on visual clues such as color changes, size, and firmness. Furthermore, modern technological innovations like sensors and data analytics are being used more frequently to precisely time harvests, which encourage productivity and resource optimization.

METHODS FOR GATHERING CELERY

With its unique crisp texture and mild flavor, celery is a popular vegetable that needs to be harvested carefully to maintain its quality. When harvesting celery, use sharp shears or knives to clip the stalks from the base of the plant. When harvesting, you mustn't bruise or injure the fragile stalks. Celery can be picked several times during its growth cycle, which enables a spaced-out and extended harvest season. Accuracy is essential since ineffective harvesting can result in shortened shelf lives and lower-quality products. Sophisticated farms frequently use equipment made especially for harvesting celery, which expedites the procedure and reduces the need for personnel.

AFTER-HARVEST MANAGEMENT AND PRESERVATION:

The treatment of harvested produce after harvest is essential to preserving its quality and freshness. Fruits and vegetables are vulnerable to several things after harvesting, including physical damage, microbial development, and moisture loss. To slow down physiological processes and increase the shelf life of perishables, rapid cooling is a frequent method. For some crops, controlled atmospheres and modified atmospheric packaging are state-of-the-art methods used to control the temperature, humidity, and gas composition while in storage. In addition, loss prevention and guaranteeing that only superior goods reach consumers are further enhanced by appropriate packing, sorting, and grading.

MEASURES FOR QUALITY CONTROL:

Sustaining quality throughout the post-harvest phase is essential to fulfilling market demands and consumer expectations. The gathered produce is carefully inspected, sorted, and graded as part of quality control procedures. To identify internal flaws or anomalies that are not immediately apparent, sophisticated technologies like spectroscopic and imaging systems are used in addition to visual and sensory assessments.

To stop infections and pollutants from growing, it is essential to follow proper sanitation procedures when handling and storing materials. Packaging is another area where quality control is used. Here, clean, contaminant-free materials enhance the product's overall safety and appeal. Maintaining the market reputation of agricultural products requires constant observation and strict adherence to quality standards.

CHAPTER SEVEN

NEW INNOVATIONS AND TRENDS

UTILIZING TECHNOLOGY IN CELERY FARMING

Technology has completely changed the agricultural industry in the last few years, and celery farming is no different. Celery farming has included precision farming methods to increase yield and efficiency. Precision seeders and transplanters—automated devices that ensure consistent crop spacing—have supplanted labor-intensive manual techniques in the planting process. In addition, real-time monitoring of soil properties, moisture content, and nutrient content is made possible by sensor-based technologies, which empower farmers to make informed decisions for the best possible crop growth.

Drone technological improvements are contributing significantly to celery farming in addition to precision farming. Drones with high-resolution cameras and sensors can take detailed pictures of celery fields, which may be used to spot possible problems like insect infestations or disease outbreaks and provide important information about the health of the crop. Farmers may apply focused treatments with this data-driven strategy, which lessens the need for broad-spectrum pesticides and encourages sustainable farming methods.

SUSTAINABLE PRACTICES AND IMPROVEMENTS

As the world moves toward more environmentally friendly agriculture, improvements have been made to minimize environmental effects while maintaining food security. Sustainable farming methods are becoming more popular in celery farming, with an emphasis on conservation and resource efficiency. The adoption of organic farming techniques, which forgo synthetic fertilizers and pesticides in favor of natural substitutes, is one noteworthy development. This meets the increasing demand from consumers for organic products while also helping the environment by lowering chemical runoff.

In addition, sustainable irrigation techniques are being used to deal with the problem of water scarcity. For example, drip irrigation systems maximize water use by supplying water straight to the base of the celery plants, reducing waste. Incorporating cover crops into celery farming enhances soil health by mitigating erosion and serves as an organic weed suppressant, hence decreasing the requirement for herbicides.

Celery farming is also embracing the concepts of the circular economy. The usage of biodegradable mulches and packaging materials is indicative of efforts to promote recycling and minimize waste. Celery growers are improving their operations' long-term viability and helping to conserve the environment by implementing these innovative and sustainable strategies.

STAYING UP TO DATE WITH SECTOR TRENDS

Celery producers need to stay up to date on industry trends to be competitive and adjust to shifting consumer needs. This is where technology comes into play, giving farmers instant access to weather forecasts, market data, and cutting-edge agricultural technologies. Farmers may connect with buyers, keep an eye on prices, and decide when to sow or harvest using mobile applications and internet platforms.

Another good option for celery growers to keep up with the current trends is to attend industry conferences and workshops. These gatherings offer chances to network with professionals, exchange stories, and learn about new developments in the field. In addition to facilitating knowledge exchange, cooperation with research institutes and agricultural extension services enables farmers to take advantage of the most recent research findings and best practices.

Farmers must pursue continual education and training in addition to technology and networking strategies to adjust to changing market trends.

www.ingramcontent.com/pod-product-compliance
Lightning Source LLC
Chambersburg PA
CBHW070842290526
45795CB00002B/949